THE BOOK OF...

HOW?

P9-CAB-484

KINGFISHER
NEW YORK

KINGFISHER
LONDON & NEW YORK

Copyright © 2010 by Kingfisher
Published in the United States by Kingfisher,
175 Fifth Ave., New York, NY 10010
Kingfisher is an imprint of Macmillan Children's Books, London.
All rights reserved.

Illustrated by Ray Bryant
Concept by Jo Connor

Distributed in the U.S. by Macmillan, 175 Fifth Ave., New York, NY 10010
Distributed in Canada by H.B. Fenn and Company Ltd., 34 Nixon Road,
Bolton, Ontario L7E 1W2

LIBRARY OF CONGRESS CATALOGING–IN–PUBLICATION DATA
The book of—how? / [illustrated by Ray Bryant].
        p. cm.
    1.   Science—Miscellanea—Juvenile literature.   I. Bryant, Ray, ill.
II. Kingfisher (Firm)
    Q173.B6754 2010
    500—dc22

                                        2010004745

ISBN: 978-0-7534-6398-7

    Kingfisher books are available for special promotions and premiums.
    For details contact: Special Markets Department, Macmillan,
        175 Fifth Avenue, New York, NY 10010.

    For more information, please visit www.kingfisherbooks.com

        First published in 2010
        Printed in China
        10 9 8 7 6 5 4 3 2
        2TR/0410/LFA/UNT/140GSM/C

WHAT'S IN THIS BOOK?

HOW . . .

HAVE YOU EVER ASKED YOURSELF HOW?

It's only natural to be confused by the world around us . . . It is a very complicated and surprising place sometimes! And you'll never understand what's going on around you unless you ask yourself "HOW?" every now and again.

This is "how" we have made this book.

We have traveled over the land, under the sea, up mountains, across deserts—and even into outer space—to collect as many tricky questions as we could find . . .

. . . and we also found the answers for you!

We now invite you to come with us on our journey around the world of "HOW," so that we can show you all the answers we discovered.

Did you know . . .

A dog's sense of smell can be up to one million times more sensitive than a human's.

While we were searching for all those answers, we found out some other pretty interesting things, too. We wrote them all down on these panels—so you can memorize these facts and impress your friends!

We also thought it might be fun to see how much of this shiny new knowledge you can remember—so at the back of the book, on pages 56 and 57, you'll find some Quick-Quiz questions to test you. It's not as scary as it sounds—we promise it'll be fun. (And besides, we've given you all the answers on pages 58 and 59.)

Are you ready for this big adventure? Then let's go!

HOW DID ANCIENT EGYPTIANS PRESERVE THEIR DEAD?

Did you know . . .

Monkeys, crocodiles, cats, and other sacred animals were often mummified, too!

A mummy is a dead body that has been wrapped in bandages. Mummies from ancient Egypt lasted for thousands of years. First, the insides of the body were removed and it was left to dry out for 40 days in salty stuff called natron. Then it was washed, rubbed with ointments, and tightly bandaged.

HOW QUICKLY CAN YOU SAIL AROUND THE WORLD?

Did you know . . .

In 1960, the U.S. Navy nuclear submarine Triton became the first craft to travel around the world entirely underwater.

The quickest time in which a boat has sailed around the world without stopping is 50 days, 16 hours, and 20 minutes. This record was achieved in March 2005 by the French sailor Bruno Peyron and his crew of 13 on board the giant catamaran Orange 2.

HOW HOT IS THE SUN?

Like all stars, the Sun is a huge ball of burning gas. It is hottest in the middle, where temperatures reach 27 million °F (15 million °C)!

Did you know . . .

We can't see Earth's atmosphere because the gases in it are invisible. On Mars, the atmosphere is full of red dust, so the sky looks orangey-brown.

HOW IS THE ATMOSPHERE LIKE A GREENHOUSE?

It gets very warm in a greenhouse, as the walls and roof keep heat from escaping. Gases in our atmosphere trap heat in a similar way and keep Earth warm. They are called greenhouse gases.

HOW MANY STARS ARE THERE?

There are about 200 billion stars in our galaxy, the Milky Way. Astronomers have figured out that there are around 1,000 billion billion stars in about 100 billion galaxies!

Did you know...

There are four main galaxy shapes: irregular (no special shape), elliptical (egg-shaped), and barred spiral. The Milky Way is a barred spiral galaxy.

HOW DO WE KNOW ABOUT THINGS IN SPACE?

Did you know . . .

The spacecraft Voyager 2 left Earth in 1977 and reached the planet Neptune 12 years later, in 1989.

Astronomers look through powerful telescopes to record what is happening in space. Astronauts, spacecraft, and robotic vehicles also travel into space to try to discover new things.

HOW FAST DO SPACE ROCKETS GO?

Did you know . . .

The tallest rocket ever launched was *Saturn V*, which blasted the *Apollo 11* spacecraft into orbit. The *Apollo 11* astronauts were the first people to land on the Moon.

Rockets have to go faster than 7 miles (11 kilometers) per second to get into space. This works out to about 24,850 (40,000 kilometers) per hour. Rockets have to travel at this speed to escape the enormously strong pull of Earth's gravity.

HOW MANY PLANETS ARE THERE?

NEPTUNE

JUPITER

MERCURY

URANUS

VENUS

SATURN

MARS

EARTH

Earth is one of eight planets that revolve around the Sun. The Sun and everything that travels around it is called the solar system. Besides the Sun and the planets, the solar system includes moons, dwarf planets, asteroids, and comets.

Did you know . . .

 Comets are like huge, dirty snowballs. Most stay on the edge of the solar system, but a few travel close to the Sun. When the Sun's heat starts to melt them, comets grow two tails—one made of gas and one made of dust.

HOW OLD IS EARTH?

Scientists think that Earth and the Moon formed about 4.6 billion years ago. Humans, though, have only been around for about 200,000 of those years.

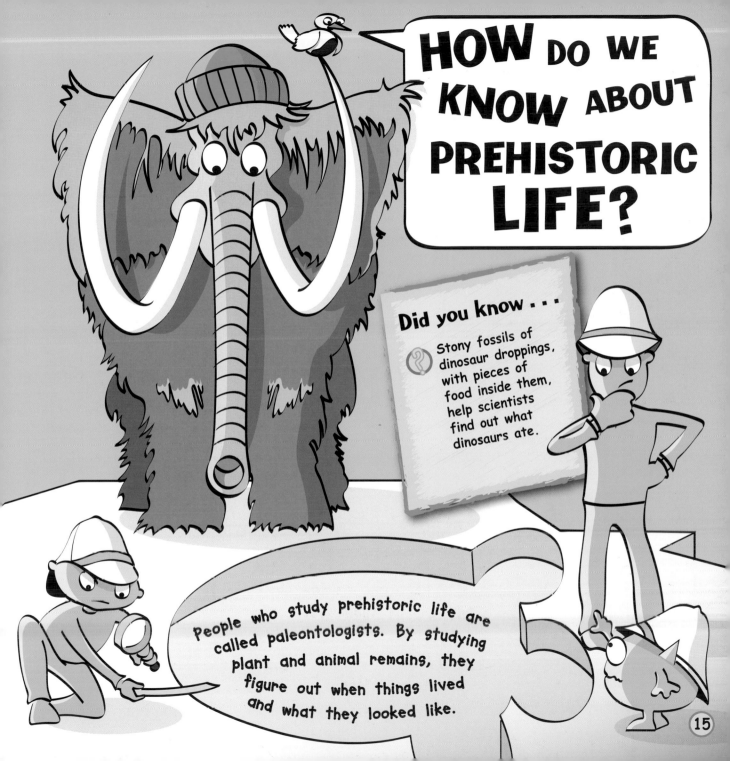

HOW DO WE KNOW ABOUT PREHISTORIC LIFE?

Did you know . . .

Stony fossils of dinosaur droppings, with pieces of food inside them, help scientists find out what dinosaurs ate.

People who study prehistoric life are called paleontologists. By studying plant and animal remains, they figure out when things lived and what they looked like.

15

Away from
the shore, the
ocean plunges
to about 2.5 miles
(4 kilometers) in most
places. The deep sea is
inky black and is colder
than a refrigerator. But
these are the perfect conditions
for some marine creatures.

HOW DEEP IS THE OCEAN?

Did you know . . .

The Scottish mountain Ben Nevis
is 4,409 feet (1,344 meters)
high. Three of these mountains
on top of each other would fit
under the sea.

HOW HIGH IS THE SKY?

The sky is part of an invisible "skin" of air around Earth. This skin is called the atmosphere, and it reaches out into space for about 300 miles (500 kilometers).

Did you know . . .

The atmosphere contains a very important gas called oxygen. All living things need oxygen in order to stay alive.

HOW OFTEN DOES IT RAIN IN THE RAINFOREST?

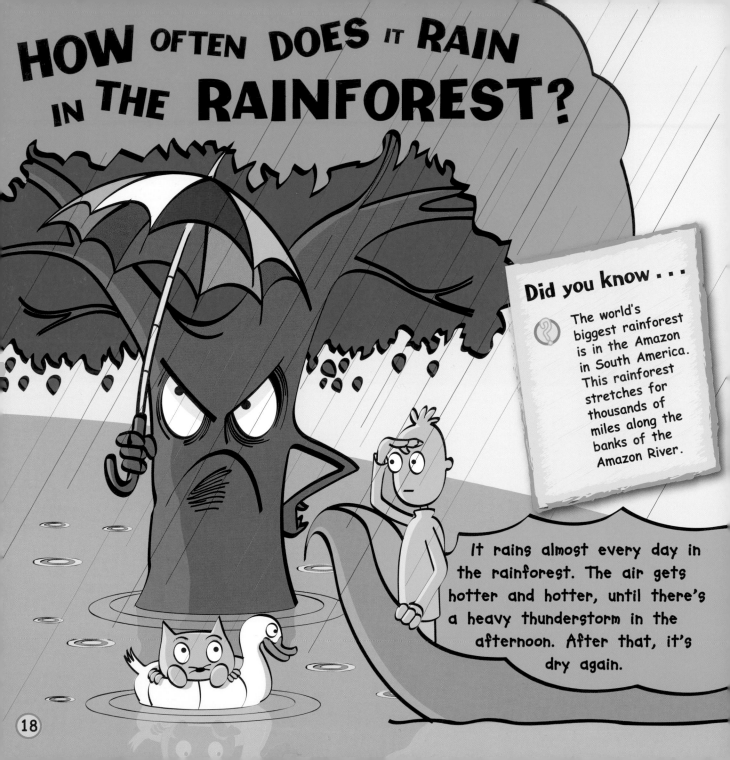

Did you know . . .

The world's biggest rainforest is in the Amazon in South America. This rainforest stretches for thousands of miles along the banks of the Amazon River.

It rains almost every day in the rainforest. The air gets hotter and hotter, until there's a heavy thunderstorm in the afternoon. After that, it's dry again.

Did you know . . .

About one-third of Earth's land is covered in forest.

HOW DO FORESTS HELP US BREATHE?

Like other animals, we breathe in oxygen from the air and breathe out carbon dioxide. Trees help us because they take in carbon dioxide and give off lots of oxygen.

19

HOW ARE CAVES MADE?

Did you know . . .

Wreckers were people who shone lights to trick ships into crashing on the rocks. They stole all the valuable things on board and hid them in caves.

Ocean waves hurl sand and rocks against a cliff face. This action by the sea slowly wears away the rock. The waves scoop out a small hollow and then a deeper hole. After a very long time, the hole is worn into a dark, damp cave.

Did you know . . .

Not all sea creatures can breathe underwater. Sea cows, seals, and dolphins breathe air, so they have to keep coming to the surface to breathe it in.

HOW DO FISH BREATHE UNDERWATER?

Unlike humans, who breathe oxygen from the air, fish breathe oxygen from the water. They gulp in water and push it out through slits in the side of their bodies, called gills. Inside the gills, oxygen passes from the water into the fish's bloodstream.

HOW DO SHARKS FIND THEIR FOOD?

Sharks can smell blood in the water
hundreds of yards away. They can also
sense the small amounts of electricity
that are given off by all living things.

23

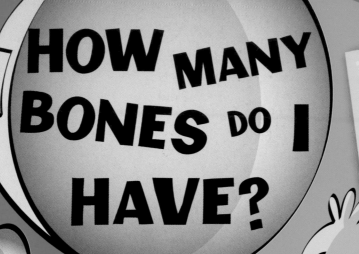

HOW MANY BONES DO I HAVE?

Did you know . . .

Bones are partly made of a hard, stonelike stuff called calcium. Food such as cheese and milk contain calcium, which helps you keep your bones strong and healthy.

Babies have about 350 bones, but adults have just over 200! This is because some of the smaller bones join together to make bigger ones as babies get older.

HOW DO WE MEASURE EARTHQUAKES?

Did you know . . .

Laser beams are used to measure ground movements and help warn people when an earthquake is coming.

An instrument called a seismometer is used to measure the vibrations of the ground during an earthquake. A pen records the vibrations on paper that is wrapped around a turning drum. The pen is attached to a weight and stays still during the earthquake, while the drum bounces around.

OW DO WAVES GET AS TALL AS A HOUSE?

Earthquakes and volcanic eruptions can cause huge waves to form out at sea. These tsunamis can travel up to 500 miles (800 kilometers) per hour.

Did you know . . .

Some volcanoes erupt continuously. Kilauea in Hawaii has been active since 1983, throwing out 177 cubic feet (5 cubic meters) of lava every second.

HOW DOES WATER CYCLE?

Water moves in a cycle. Tree roots soak up rainwater when it falls. The water moves to the leaves and is released into the air as vapor. This rises and turns into clouds. When it rains, the cycle starts again.

Did you know . . .

The rainiest place in the world is Mount Waialeale in Hawaii. It rains there for about 350 days every year!

HOW DO PLANTS SURVIVE IN THE DESERT?

Did you know . . .

When desert plants do get water, they hang on to it. Some use their leaves like a water bank, storing the water until it is needed. Cacti store it in their fat, juicy stems.

All living things need water in order to survive. Desert plants slurp up water through their roots, which are very long and reach deep into the ground.

HOW IS WIND FARMED?

Did you know . . .

Some power plants burn crops such as straw and elephant grass to make electricity.

The first wind-powered machines were windmills. Today, turbines are used to catch the wind at wind farms on land and out at sea. The wind is used to generate electricity.

HOW DO MOUNTAINS FORM?

Did you know . . .

A volcano is a type of mountain. It occurs when there is an opening in Earth's crust. Hot ash, gas, and liquid rock, called lava, are forced up through the volcano from deep inside Earth.

The movements made by Earth's plates are powerful enough to make mountains. Different movements form three types of mountains—fold, volcanic, and block.

31

HOW DO WE KNOW WHAT DINOSAURS LOOKED LIKE?

Did you know . . .

Putting together a dinosaur fossil is like doing a puzzle, and it's easy to make a mistake. Scientists first thought that an Iguanodon's thumb spike was a horn on its nose!

Scientists reconstruct a dinosaur skeleton using fossilized bones. They imagine what a dinosaur looked like by studying modern animals, such as reptiles.

OW DO WE KNOW ABOUT ANCIENT PEOPLE?

Did you know . . .

One of the most famous historical discoveries was the tomb of the Egyptian pharaoh Tutankhamen. The tomb had lain undiscovered for more than 3,000 years!

Archaeologists study remains from the ancient world, such as buildings, tools, jewelry, and coins. They look for clues in an object that might tell them how old it is, who made it, and why it was found in that particular place.

HOW DO THINGS APPEAR ON TV?

Your TV set has an antenna for receiving television signals, and the TV turns these into sounds and pictures. These signals are sent out by tall transmitters and bounced around the planet using satellites in orbit around Earth.

Did you know . . .

Television signals are carried into space by radio waves. They travel at about 186,400 miles (300,000 kilometers) per hour. Signals are sent up and beamed back to TV sets in just seconds!

HOW DO BUBBLES GET INTO SOFT DRINKS?

The bubbles in soft drinks are made up of carbon dioxide. The gas is squashed into the bottle so tightly that it disappears into the drink. When the bottle is opened, the bubbles have space to escape and start fizzing into the air.

Did you know . . .

Carbon dioxide is present in baking powder, which is used to make cakes rise. When a cake mixture is heated, bubbles of carbon dioxide form. The bubbles get bigger, and this makes the cake rise.

HOW LONG DOES A TREE LIVE?

Did you know . . .

Trees make new wood every year and leave a telltale ring in their trunk. Counting the rings on a tree stump tells you how old the tree was when it was felled (cut down).

Trees grow very slowly and have long lives. Most trees live between 100 and 200 years, but some types of pine trees are more than 4,500 years old! They are some of the oldest living things on Earth.

HOW CAN YOU TELL A HORSE'S AGE?

Did you know . . .

Horses have to see a dentist for a checkup at least twice a year.

Horses mainly eat grass, and munching away at this tough plant food is very hard on teeth. Experts can get a good idea of a horse's age by looking at the way its teeth are wearing as it gets older.

HOW DO DIVERS STAY WARM?

Divers wear wetsuits in cold water to help them stay warm. The wetsuits are made of rubber, which stops body heat from escaping as quickly as it would normally.

Did you know . . .

A thin layer of water is trapped between a diver's wetsuit and his body. The diver's body heat warms this layer, and the rubber wetsuit keeps the heat from escaping.

The Sun's rays are much stronger out in space than they are on Earth, so astronauts wear a suit of stretchy underwear to keep them cool. Tiny plastic tubes carry cool water through the underwear, taking away body heat and helping the astronaut stay cool.

Did you know . . .

Space shuttles need to stay cool as well. Special tiles insulate the shuttle and keep it from getting too hot.

HOW DO SPIDERS MAKE THREAD?

Spiders make silk inside their bodies, drawing it out through little knobs on their bodies called spinnerets. On contact with the air, the silk sets into a thread, which the spider then weaves into a web, using its spinnerets like fingers.

HOW DO PEOPLE CLIMB MOUNTAINS?

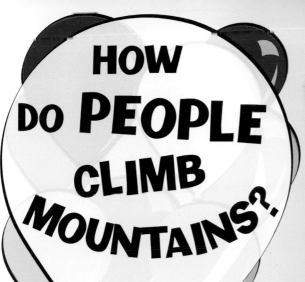

Did you know . . .

The first woman to climb to the top of Mount Everest was Junko Tabei, of Japan, on May 16, 1975.

Mountain climbers use special equipment to help them clamber up rock faces and protect them from falls. Ropes are a climber's lifeline—one end goes around the climber's waist, and the other is looped through metal spikes called pitons. The climber hammers the pitons into the rock as he or she moves upward.

Did you know . . .

Deathwatch beetles like to munch through floorboards, and they attract a mate by tapping their jaws. People once thought that this knocking was a sign that someone in the house was about to die.

The male meadow grasshopper plays its body like a violin. It uses its back legs like a bow, scraping them against its wings to make a loud "chirruping" sound. It does this to attract a mate or to warn off other males.

HOW DO SNAKES MOVE WITHOUT ANY LEGS?

One of the ways that a snake moves is by throwing its body forward in zigzags. By pushing back against stones, it forces itself forward and backward.

Did you know . . .

Snakes can bend and twist because their backbone is made of hundreds of tiny bones, all linked together like a chain.

HOW LONG CAN A CAMEL GO WITHOUT WATER?

Did you know . . .

There are two types of camels. Arabian camels have one hump, while Bactrian camels of Asia have two.

Camels can survive for days without water—or for weeks if they find enough juicy plants to eat. When a camel drinks, it can gulp down 26 gallons (100 liters) in ten minutes.

HOW DO PEOPLE SURVIVE IN THE DESERT?

Did you know . . .

Most nomads keep their own herds, so they can drink the animals' milk or make the milk into cheese.

Desert survival is all about finding enough water and food to stay alive. Some people who live in the desert move from place to place all the time, following good sources of food and water. These traveling people are called nomads.

HOW DO BATS SEE IN THE DARK?

Bats can fly and find food in total darkness. They do this by using sound waves. Bats make high-pitched sounds, which bounce off solid objects and back to the bats. This means that bats can avoid bumping into things in the dark.

Did you know . . .

Vampire bats are the only mammals that feed entirely on blood. They live in groups of about 100, and one colony can drink the blood of 25 cows in a year!

HOW DO I KNOW WHAT'S GOING ON?

Did you know . . .

A dog's sense of smell can be up to one million times more sensitive than a human's. This is why the police use dogs to help them detect things that are hidden from view.

You have five senses. They are sight, hearing, smell, touch, and taste. Using information from your sense organs—such as your eyes, ears, nose, and tongue—your brain learns about the world around you.

HOW HIGH CAN A KANGAROO HOP?

Did you know . . .

A flea can jump more than 100 times its own height!

A large kangaroo can jump right over your head! The highest that a kangaroo has ever jumped is about 10 feet (3 meters). Their big, strong back legs help kangaroos to be such good jumpers.

HOW FAST CAN A CHEETAH RUN?

Did you know . . .

Cheetahs use their sharp claws to grip and push against the ground as they race along. Olympic runners have spikes on their shoes for the same reason.

A hungry cheetah can sprint faster than 60 miles (100 kilometers) per hour when it is chasing something to eat. But running this fast soon tires out the cheetah, and it has to stop to get its breath back.

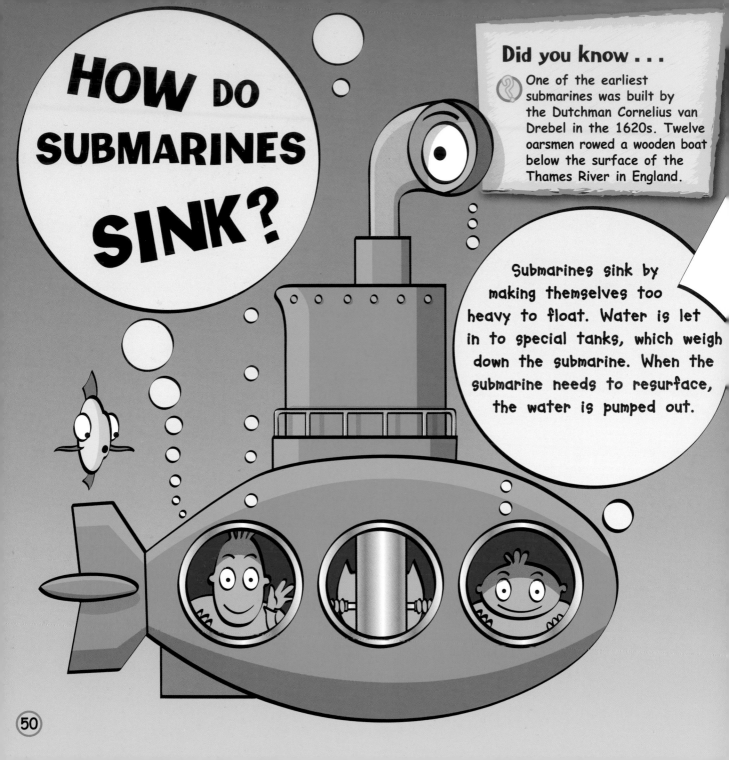

HOW DO YOU RIDE ON AIR?

People ride on air every time they travel by hovercraft. The hovercraft was invented by the Englishman Christopher Cockerell in 1959. He discovered that trapping a cushion of air beneath a boat lifts it up above the waves, allowing it to travel much faster.

HOW DO BIRDS FLY?

Did you know . . .
Hummingbirds are the only birds that can fly backward. They can also fly forward, sideways, and upside-down.

When birds flap their wings up and down, they are pushing themselves through the air. This gets tiring after a while, so they save energy by gliding and let the air currents carry them along.

HOW DO BIRDS KNOW WHERE TO GO?

Did you know . . .

It gets so cold in Antarctica that some penguins migrate north to South America. They don't fly, of course—they swim!

In the fall, the days become cooler and shorter. This is a signal to migrating birds that it will soon be time to leave to go somewhere warmer. They use the Sun, stars, and landmarks to fly in the right direction.

HOW MANY COUNTRIES ARE THERE?

There are just under 200 official countries in the world, each one with its own laws and leaders. But this number can change. This is because new countries are sometimes made. For example, a country might split up into several smaller ones.

QUICK-QUIZ QUESTIONS

1. How long does it take for the Sun's light to reach Earth?

2. Unscramble HERE US GONE SAGES to show which atmospheric gases trap heat.

3. Appoximately how many stars are there in our galaxy?

4. Why do space rockets have to travel so fast?

5. Other than the Sun and the planets, what else is in the solar system?

6. How long have humans been on Earth?

7. What gas do all living things need in order to stay alive?

8. Where is the world's largest rainforest?

9. What does "TBM" stand for?

10. Fish breathe oxygen from water, not air. True or false?

11. What are bones partly made of?

12. What are tendons?

20. What do divers wear to help them stay warm?

21. What are the two types of camels?

13. Unscramle SEMI METEORS to show an instrument that measures earthquakes.

14. How fast can a tsunami travel?

22. How many senses do you have?

23. When was one of the first submarines built?

24. Unscramble CRAVE FORTH to show what travels across water quickly.

15. Straw and elephant grass can make electricity. True or false?

16. What are the three types of mountains?

17. Which Egyptian pharaoh's tomb lay undiscovered for more than 3,000 years?

25. What is the largest country in the world?

18. Which gas creates the bubbles in soft drinks?

19. What age can some pine trees reach?

QUICK-QUIZ ANSWERS

1. 8.3 minutes.

2. HERE US GONE SAGES = greenhouse gases.

3. About 200 billion.

4. To escape the pull of Earth's gravity.

5. Moons, dwarf planets, asteroids, and comets.

6. About 200,000 years.

7. Oxygen.

8. The Amazon Rainforest is in South America.

9. Tunnel-boring machine.

10. True.

11. A hard, stonelike stuff called calcium.

12. Strong, white, stringy things that attach muscles to bones.

13. SEMI METEORS = seismometer.

14. Up to 500 miles (800 kilometers) per hour.

15. True. Some power plants burn them to make electricity.

16. Fold, volcanic, and block.

17. Tutankhamen's.

18. Carbon dioxide.

19. More than 4,500 years old.

20. Wetsuits.

21. Arabian camels and Bactrian camels.

22. Five.

23. In the 1620s.

24. CRAVE FORTH = hovercraft.

25. Russia.

TRICKY WORDS

CARBON DIOXIDE
A colorless, invisible gas that animals exhale (breathe out). Plants absorb it as they grow. Carbon dioxide is also produced by burning fossil fuels, such as coal and oil.

CATAMARAN
A boat with two hulls, or bodies, joined together so that they are parallel to each other (side by side).

COMET
An object made up of ice, dust, and small rocks that orbits the Sun. Unlike asteroids, comets usually have two "tails"—one made up of dust and one of gas.

FOSSIL
The remains of a plant or creature that existed long ago. Fossils are usually formed from the hard parts of an animal or plant, such as teeth, bones, or shells. They are created when, for example, animal bones sink into mud, which then gradually hardens into rock.

GALAXY
A huge system of millions or billions of stars. The stars, together with gas and dust, are held together by the force of gravity.

GRAVITY
A force of attraction between objects. This happens in space, for example, where a moon is held in orbit around a planet, because the planet has a larger mass.

GREENHOUSE GASES
Gases in Earth's atmosphere that contribute to the greenhouse effect, or global warming. Greenhouse gases include carbon dioxide, nitrous oxide, methane, and ozone.

HOVERCRAFT
A boat that travels across water on a cushion of air.

AIR CURRENT
Moving air caused by differences in temperature or air pressure.

ARCHAEOLOGIST
Someone whose job it is to find out about human history by recovering and studying remains, such as buildings and clothing.

ASTEROID
An object made up of rock and metal orbiting (traveling around) the Sun, left over from when the solar system was formed.

ASTRONOMER
A scientist whose job it is to study the planets, stars, and galaxies.

ATMOSPHERE
The layer of gases surrounding a planet. Earth's atmosphere keeps in heat from the Sun but also keeps out many harmful rays from the Sun.

INSULATE
To cover with material in order to keep warm.

LAVA
Liquid rock that spurts from volcanoes or cracks in Earth's surface.

MIGRATE
To move from one place to another according to the changing seasons.

NATRON
A type of salt found at the bottom of dried-up lakes.

ORBIT
The path of an object as it travels around something. Earth orbits the Sun.

OXYGEN
A colorless, invisible gas in air that animals need to breathe in order to live.

PALEONTOLOGIST
Someone whose job it is to find out about prehistoric life by studying the fossilized remains of plants and animals, such as dinosaurs.

PREY
An animal that is hunted and eaten by another animal.

SENSOR
A part of an animal's body that collects information for a particular sense, such as taste or smell.

SEWERAGE
The system of drains used to carry sewage (human waste and waste water).

SOLAR SYSTEM
The Sun and the objects in space that orbit it, including the eight planets.

SPACE SHUTTLE
A spacecraft that carries astronauts on space missions.

SPINNERET
A spider's silk-spinning organ, usually found on the underside of its body. Most spiders have six spinnerets.

TRANSMITTER
A device that changes a signal into radio waves that can travel through space. The signal can travel long distances and can be received by a machine, such as a television.

TUNNEL-BORING MACHINE
Gigantic drill-like machines that twist and grind their way through the ground to make large tunnels.

TURBINE
A tall machine with long blades that turn in the wind to capture its energy. This wind energy is converted into electricity.

VAPOR
A mass of tiny drops of water in the air that appears as mist or steam.

WATER CYCLE
The "journey" of water as it rises and turns into clouds in the sky and then falls back to the ground as rain.

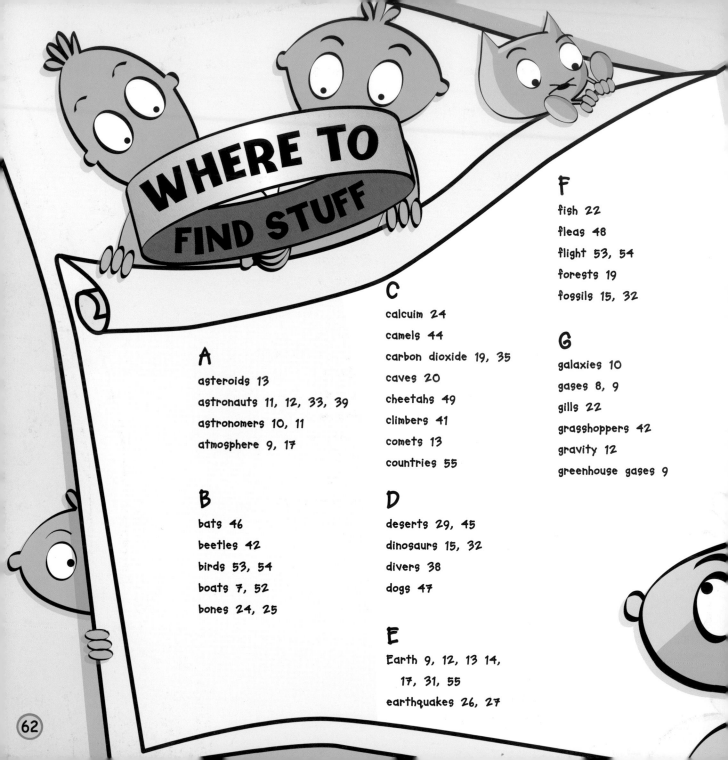

WHERE TO FIND STUFF

Wow! What an amazing journey! We hope you had as much fun as we did and learned many new things. Who knew that there was so much to discover about "how!" Speaking of "who," we can tell you that we'll soon be going on a few more exciting journeys:

The Book of . . . Why?
The Book of . . . What?
The Book of . . . Who?

Look out for these great books!
"Who" knows "what" we'll discover . . .

See you soon!